# Set Your Boundaries Your Way

## No Guilt, No Games, No Drama

STEPH STERNER

Copyright © 2012 – 2017 Stephanie J Sterner

ISBN-10: 1542739292
ISBN-13: 978-1542739290

All rights reserved.

Neither this book nor any part of it may be reproduced in any form without written permission. The only exception is brief passages contained in reviews and articles where the author and title are mentioned.

Neither the author nor the publisher shall be liable for any loss, injury or damage allegedly arising from the use or misuse of this information.

We are all responsible for the choices we make in our lives, regardless of where our ideas come from. It is always up to you what to say, how to say it and whether to say it at all. The purpose of this book is to help you to understand your options so that you can make better choices.

# MORE BOOKS BY STEPH STERNER

*7 Easy Ways to Say NO to Almost Anyone:*
*Stand Up for Yourself Without Looking (or Feeling)*
*Unreasonable, Uncaring or Unkind*

Cat got your tongue? No problem! This book will show you how to say *no* to all kinds of people and situations. When you know how to set your boundaries gracefully, you're able to respect both yourself and others. And with a plenty of options for so many situations, you're sure to find something that works for you.

## COMING SOON

*Where Did I Go?*
*The Insider's Guide to Better Boundaries*

If you struggle with boundaries and you'd like to understand yourself better, this is your book. The focus is on you and the limiting beliefs, behaviors and emotional patterns that have been holding you back.

All of Steph Sterner's books are available on stephsterner.com

# DEDICATION

This book is dedicated to everyone who finds it difficult to set boundaries. Maybe someone is manipulating you. Maybe you're simply "too nice." Whatever the reason, I hope you find the courage to do what's right for you.

# ACKNOWLEDGMENTS

I'd like to thank everyone who has believed in me and supported me throughout my life. I am grateful for all the support I've received, especially from my parents and my amazing partner. I couldn't do it without you!

# TABLE OF CONTENTS

| | |
|---|---|
| Preface: What You Can Expect from This Book | 1 |
| Better Boundaries | 5 |
| The First Key: Know Yourself | 11 |
| YOUR VALUES | 11 |
| YOUR BELIEFS | 12 |
| YOUR UNIQUE STRENGTHS & WEAKNESSES | 14 |
| FEEL GOOD ABOUT YOURSELF | 14 |
| The Second Key: Know Others | 17 |
| YOUR FEELINGS | 18 |
| RESPONSIBILITY & OBLIGATION | 19 |
| REASONABLE VS UNREASONABLE PEOPLE | 20 |
| AUTHORITY | 25 |
| TAKE YOUR TIME | 27 |
| The Third Key: Understand the Consequences of Not Setting a Boundary | 28 |
| 1. YOU MAY BE THE ONLY ONE WHO SEES IT THAT WAY | 28 |
| 2. THE EXPECTATIONS DON'T END HERE | 29 |
| 3. YOU EXHAUST YOURSELF | 29 |
| 4. YOU LOSE THE RESPECT OF OTHERS | 30 |
| 5. YOU LOSE YOUR SELF-RESPECT | 31 |

| | |
|---|---|
| 6. You feel angry and resentful | 31 |
| 7. You lose your integrity | 32 |
| 8. You say no to something important | 33 |
| Remember ... | 33 |

## The Fourth Key: Know What's Missing — 35

| | |
|---|---|
| The True Size of the Task | 35 |
| Recurring Problems | 36 |
| The Involvement of Others | 37 |
| The Money | 37 |
| Invisible Obligations | 38 |
| Unexpected Challenges | 40 |
| Why You? | 41 |
| A Brief Reminder | 41 |

## The Fifth Key: Stamp Out Those Lies — 43

| | |
|---|---|
| I have an obligation. | 43 |
| But then I won't be a good person. | 46 |
| Their needs are more important. | 47 |
| When you love someone, it's up to you to make that person happy. | 49 |
| This little thing isn't worth fighting over. | 50 |
| It's better to keep the peace. | 52 |
| There's nothing I can do. | 53 |
| It's no big deal. I shouldn't feel so angry. | 55 |
| They just can't manage without me. | 57 |
| I can't handle the consequences. | 58 |

| | |
|---|---|
| BUT THEY WON'T LIKE ME. | 60 |
| I CAN NEVER BREAK MY WORD. | 61 |
| THERE ARE SOME PEOPLE I JUST CAN'T SAY NO TO. | 62 |
| THEY JUST WON'T TAKE NO FOR AN ANSWER. | 64 |
| WHAT ARE YOU BELIEVING? | 66 |

## The 6th Key: Recognize the Emotions that Stop You in Your Tracks    67

| | |
|---|---|
| FEAR OF SAYING NO | 68 |
| FEAR OF CONFLICT | 69 |
| FEAR OF REJECTION | 70 |
| FEAR OF REJECTION | 70 |
| CRAVING THE APPROVAL OF OTHERS | 71 |
| NEED TO BE NEEDED | 73 |
| GUILT | 75 |
| FEELING SORRY FOR SOMEONE | 78 |
| LONELINESS | 79 |
| ALL THOSE EMOTIONS | 79 |

## The 7th Key: The Power of Acceptance    81

| | |
|---|---|
| ACCEPT YOURSELF | 82 |
| ACCEPT YOUR EMOTIONS | 83 |
| ACCEPT OTHERS' CHOICES | 85 |
| ACCEPT OTHERS' OPINIONS OF YOU | 86 |
| ACCEPT, ACCEPT, ACCEPT | 87 |

## Some Final Words: Decide for Yourself    89

| What's next? | 93 |
|---|---|
| About the Author | 94 |

# PREFACE

# WHAT YOU CAN EXPECT FROM THIS BOOK

Do you wonder when to stand up for yourself … and when to keep quiet and "suck it up"? Or does your gut tell you it's high time for a boundary, but you're not sure what it should be? Maybe you don't hear that little whisper … and you get blindsided by a convincing argument or your own emotional patterns.

Setting better boundaries can be a challenge. After all, good people sacrifice for others – but smart people make sure their own needs are met. There are so many things to consider when choosing a boundary:

- your values and beliefs about the situation;
- the type of person or people you're dealing with;
- the consequences of not setting a boundary;
- the potential for missing or inaccurate information;
- the many lies that run around in your head, persuading you to give away your power;
- the painful emotions, such as guilt and shame, that we all try so hard to avoid; and
- the need to accept others' choices as well as your own limitations.

With all of this to consider, it's easy to feel overwhelmed. That's one of the reasons we tend to nod our heads and go along. But unless we know where to draw the line, we can end up feeling resentful and unfulfilled. That resentment eats away at our relationships, and putting ourselves last destroys our self-esteem.

I know this because I used to be a bit of a doormat. I felt terribly uncomfortable refusing even unreasonable requests. I didn't understand the games people were playing – or the consequences of my choices. Since then I've spent years researching the many aspects of boundaries: everything from the tactics people use to the emotional patterns that keep us stuck. And I learned that awareness is the key. If someone had explained these things to me when I was younger, I could have avoided a lot of pain.

That's why I wrote *Set Your Boundaries Your Way*: to help you to see what's going on in your communications and to understand the consequences of your choices. Once you see through the games, some of which may be played within your own mind, you'll be able to make decisions that work for you. Rather than backfiring later, your choices will support you in creating the life you want. Better boundaries improve your relationships, help you to feel better about yourself and make room in your life for the people and things that matter to you the most.

It was important to me to make this book as simple and practical as possible, so that you can put it to use in your life. As one reviewer put it:

"This guide is written clearly and gives straightforward examples. Unlike other self-help books I've read, this one really stuck with me, I think because the author writes so matter of factly. She doesn't spout theories or get preachy; she talks like a mother or friend would, just giving you straight-talk."

That's what would have helped me the most all those years ago: straight talk.

Setting boundaries can be intimidating when we can't see what's happening in our relationships and within ourselves. *Set Your Boundaries Your Way* takes the mystery out of your interactions, showing you what you've missed. Maybe you haven't thought about the long-term price you pay for going along. Maybe you've been making decisions without all the information you need. Maybe you're taking on someone else's problems. Or maybe you're trying to avoid difficult emotions, only to discover that they won't go away ... at least, not for long.

The purpose of boundaries is to protect your highest values. This is why setting better boundaries can transform your life. When people see that you respect yourself, they naturally respect you for it. (Those who don't usually have their own agenda, one that doesn't include you or your feelings.) When you protect what matters most to you, you feel good about yourself. And you begin to take back your life. It's impossible to describe how good this feels; it's something you have to experience for yourself.

If you've been allowing others to make your decisions, lacking the confidence to set boundaries that work for you – this is your chance. Read this book now. At less than 20,000 words, you don't need to wait until next month or next year to start (or finish!). It's simple and concise, with examples to help you relate everything to your own life.

Read as much or as little as you want – and let it roll around in your subconscious. Pick it up again when you're ready, reading or re-reading as you like. Before you know it, you'll be seeing yourself, your relationships and your world in a whole new light. And that can change your life!

# INTRODUCTION

# BETTER BOUNDARIES

We've all struggled to set a boundary at some point in our lives. Some people are harder to say *no* to than others, and there will always be some manipulation strategies that we don't know how to deal with – or even recognize. Setting and maintaining boundaries can be hard work.

But what about the part that comes before setting the boundary? How can we be sure we've chosen the **right** boundary? Maintaining boundaries requires persistence. How do you stick to something when we're not even sure you should?

Your sister has asked you to drive her kids home from school. It's not at all convenient for you, but you can do it. She's had a tough divorce, and her ex doesn't help her much. Lately she's been asking more and more of you. Do you keep putting her needs first, or do you set some limits? How do you decide?

You've agreed to plan your parents' anniversary party. At the last minute, your sister asks you to pick up the food. You're concerned that she expects you to pay for it as well – she often makes comments about the high cost of raising children and the financial benefits of being single. As the only one in the family without children, you were happy to spend hours organizing and making sure that everyone in the family would be there. But no one consulted you about the costs, and you have other plans for your money. What now?

Your boss has asked everyone on your team to work on Saturday. You've worked every weekend for the past two months, as it seems there's always a crisis on this project. Often you've been the only team member at the office. You've made plans for Saturday, and you're looking forward to spending some time with friends. You're afraid to say *no*, but you've had enough. What do you do?

The purpose of this book is **not** to answer these questions for you. The purpose of this book is to help you find the answers for yourself. Your answers may differ from mine. If you choose mine – which are based on my values, beliefs and experience – you may end up miserable. Better boundaries are based on **your** values, **your** beliefs and **your** experience.

The keys to better boundaries are like the pieces of a puzzle. When you bring them all together, you see the whole picture. And that's when you know what to do – because you know what's right.

Here's a quick peek at those keys and why they're so important:

1. **Know yourself.** If you don't know what's most important to you, what you believe, and where your strengths and weaknesses lie, how can you make choices that work for you?
2. **Know others.** Better boundaries don't just apply to situations; they apply to people and relationships, too. Some government employees have authority over you; refusing to show up for an audit won't solve your tax problems. Some people have your best interests at heart, while others are purely self-centered. It doesn't make sense to treat them the same.
3. **Understand the consequences of not setting a boundary.** Sometimes it seems easier to "go with the flow." It's not worth rocking the boat. While that may be easier in the short-term, the consequences seldom end there. Failing to set a boundary has its price. It may mean that you sacrifice something important – or exhaust yourself trying to do it all. You lose the respect of others and, even more importantly, yourself. And you end up feeling angry and resentful toward others. Both your self-esteem and your relationships suffer.
4. **Know what's missing.** Often we agree to things before we understand how much is involved. We only realize the true size of the task once we're in the middle of it – when it's too late to say *no*. Or we may solve a problem

once, only to discover that it happens often – and everyone expects us to fix it. There may even be financial implications that we weren't aware of – or that we assumed someone else was handling. It's important to consider this and more before making a commitment.

5. **Stamp out those lies.** Sometimes we agree to things – or put up with unpleasant situations or behavior – because we think we must. Anything else would make us bad people. Their needs are more important than ours. It's better to keep the peace. It's no big deal. And besides, they'll never take *no* for an answer.

   These beliefs and more drive us to make bad decisions. It's important to recognize these lies and embrace the truth. After all, it's the truth that sets us free.

6. **Recognize the emotions that stop you in your tracks.** Some of us know exactly when to say *no* – but we're afraid to do it. We may look to others to feel loved or needed. We may be afraid of conflict or rejection. Or we may do things from a misguided sense of guilt or pity. When this happens, the first step is to understand ourselves and what's driving our decisions.

7. **Harness the power of acceptance.** When others make unreasonable demands or ignore our clearly stated boundaries, it's tempting to demand that they change. And when someone

plays the guilt card, it's easy to tell ourselves that we should be better than we are. Once you accept yourself and others, you're free to respond to their words and actions in the best way possible. Instead of demanding that they change (or wishing that you could), you can decide what to do about it.

When we place someone else's values ahead of our own, we suffer. We feel uncomfortable about our relationships and ourselves. When we do what's right for us, even if it's difficult, we feel good about ourselves and the choices we've made. And when we feel good about ourselves, we find it easier to continue doing what's right. This leads to a happier and more fulfilling life.

And that is my wish – that by applying the principles in this book, you may lead a happier and more fulfilling life.

# CHAPTER 1

# THE FIRST KEY: KNOW YOURSELF

It sounds so easy: Know yourself. How can you not? After all, you live with this person every day of your life. What's not to know?

Plenty! To choose boundaries that work for you, you need to know your values, your beliefs, and your unique strengths and weaknesses.

## Your Values

To make good decisions, you need to know what's important to you. But this is more than a list. You also need to know how much things matter, so that you can decide what to sacrifice and what to protect.

For example, let's say that family is important to you; so is spending time in nature. Your mother asks you to take her to an out-of-town church event on Saturday, the very day that the hiking club is going to your favorite place. You've been looking forward to this all-day hike for weeks, and taking your mother means giving it up. You simply cannot do both. Which is more important? How will you choose?

Of course, the decision is usually more complicated than this. There may be other family members who could take her – perhaps even some who haven't been doing their fair share with your mom. Or perhaps you haven't done much for her lately because you've been spending your weekends hiking. Maybe you and your mother aren't getting along – or maybe she's getting older, and you're worried that she won't be around much longer.

As you can see, a "simple" decision isn't always so simple. There may be many factors to consider. And if you don't know what matters most, these decisions can be tough.

## Your Beliefs

Beliefs also play an important role in our decisions. If you believe that your mother's church group is poisoning her mind with their judgments and intolerance, you may not want to take her to anything church-related. If this hike has a special meaning to you – perhaps it's the hardest one on the schedule, and you weren't fit enough for it until now – it may feel even more important. If you believe that your brother should be helping you look after your mother, you may want him to take her – even though he lives 45 minutes away and may have plans of his own.

Our beliefs about what's right and what's wrong, as well as our beliefs about other people, will naturally influence our decisions. It's when we're not aware of these beliefs or their effects on us that we have a potential problem.

There are two limiting beliefs that I'd like to mention here. If you believe that others' needs are more important than your own, you're likely to give up your hike without even asking for help. This belief leads us to sacrifice the things we care about – sometimes for things that mean little to others.

The second belief is like the first one: good people always put others first. If you want to see yourself as a good person, you'll continually sacrifice your time and your priorities for someone else's. And you'll make that sacrifice even when your needs seem more important than everyone else's.

---

> Your anger and resentment
> will only grow until you find
> a way to respect your own needs.

---

Know that, whether you acknowledge these feelings or not, your anger and resentment will only grow until you find a way to respect your own needs as well as others'.

## Your Unique Strengths and Weaknesses

Let's say your sister has asked you to come to her doctor's appointment. She's had some tests, and the doctor is going to tell her what's wrong and explain her options. She's nervous, and she doesn't like dealing with doctors and medical issues. She says she'll feel much more comfortable if you're there with her.

Obviously your feelings about your sister will factor into this decision. But let's look at you: your personality, what you're good at, and what you're not so good at. If you're comfortable with medical information and potentially difficult decisions about treatment, you'll probably be willing to go. If you share your sister's fear of all things medical (or you're uncomfortable questioning authority figures), you may want to suggest someone more appropriate to go with her. Your fears may only make things worse for her. And if you're the kind of person who takes on other people's problems, it could be difficult for you. Until your sister makes her decision, you may find that you've taken on a lot of stress. (But, of course, you may be willing to do it anyway.)

## Feel Good about Yourself

Knowing yourself means understanding what makes you tick. The more you know about yourself, the easier it will be to decide whether to set a boundary or simply go along. When your decisions are based on good information, they work for you.

You won't always get the results you wanted, but you'll feel comfortable knowing that you made the best decision possible.

When you don't have enough information – or fail to take something important into account – you're likely to regret your decisions. You may even feel resentful or guilty. Understanding and accepting where you're at can make all the difference in the world.

# CHAPTER 2

# THE SECOND KEY: KNOW OTHERS

Once you know yourself, you can begin to focus on others. Whenever you're considering doing a favor, putting up with bad behavior, or even asking for what you want, it pays to know the nature of the others involved. Boundaries are all about relationships, and it's a good idea to understand the dynamic before making important decisions.

Here are some questions to consider when you're contemplating the role of others in your decisions. This list is not complete, and of course not all of these questions will be relevant every time. But this should give you plenty to think about:

- How do you feel about the main person involved? Do you like and respect him or her? Are you close or distant? Is this person important in your life?
- Do you feel a sense of responsibility or obligation toward someone? If so, what is it based on? And does this person have a habit of using it against you?
- Is this person reasonable, or are you likely to be dealing with dramas and unrealistic expectations?
- Are you in a position of authority, or does someone have authority over you? If so, what is the nature of that authority? What are its limits?

## Your Feelings

Let's start with your feelings toward the other person. The central issue is his or her importance in your life. Keep in mind what someone means to you while you're deciding how much effort (or sacrifice) is appropriate. It's natural to do more for someone you like, respect or feel close to.

But what if the person's importance is not about liking, respect or closeness? What if that person has something you want – or could take away something important to you?

If you're afraid that your ex-wife will turn the kids against you unless you give her what she wants, you may find yourself at her mercy for years to come. Is this the way you want to live? And will it really guarantee you a good relationship with your children? What kind of example are you setting for them? What will their future relationships be like? After all, their parents are their first role models.

> Your good feelings about yourself
> are too precious to be traded.

Sometimes we agree to things that don't sit well with us so that we can benefit from someone's money or connections. Before you do that, think carefully about the choices you're making. The price is higher than you might think. When you act against your own values, even in what seem to be small ways, your self-esteem suffers. Your good feelings about yourself are too precious to be traded.

## Responsibility and Obligation

Whenever you feel responsible for someone else's outcomes, it's worth questioning what's going on. Is there a real responsibility here, as there would be with a child or a pet? Have you made a commitment that you must keep? Or is that sense of responsibility based on something else? Perhaps taking on others' responsibilities has become a habit. Or you think that if you don't take care of something, it won't get done.

Or someone "needs" help, and you see yourself as the one to provide it.

Be careful. Often when we take on others' responsibilities, it makes us feel needed. And many of us (especially, but not only, women) want to feel that way. Why? Because we don't feel good about ourselves unless someone depends on us. We've been taught that being a good person means serving others.

Most of us like to feel needed, and we enjoy the approval that comes with meeting someone's needs. But it's important to remember that this kind of approval only lasts until you're needed again. And the approval isn't even for you – it's for your decision to make someone happy at your own expense. You're considered a "good girl" or a "good boy" as long as you're willing to ignore your own needs.

It seems to me that what we crave is love and acceptance. Approval is just a cheap substitute. Don't sell yourself short. If you can't get the real thing from someone, maybe it's time to change the nature of that relationship – and learn to accept yourself as you are.

---

> What we crave is
> love and acceptance.
> Approval is just a cheap substitute.

---

## Reasonable vs Unreasonable People

By "unreasonable people," I'm referring to those who consistently put themselves first and expect you to do the same. These people usually won't listen to reason; many of them get aggressive when you disagree with them. They don't seem willing (or perhaps even able) to put themselves in your shoes. They may regularly break their commitments to you – assuming they've made any at all. Or they may only treat you kindly when you're agreeing with them, admiring them or doing something for them.

These people are unpleasant to deal with because they're not interested in what's important to you. Until you recognize their nature and accept that they won't change, you will continue to have unrealistic expectations of them. If you're feeling ignored, pressured or otherwise disrespected by someone – especially if this isn't the first time – ask yourself whether he or she is being reasonable.

If you're not sure, look at your past interactions. Have you felt respected? When you've expressed your needs and opinions, have you felt listened to? Were they considered? Is there a give and take in the relationship, or does it feel as though you're doing all the giving?

Most of us consider others as well as ourselves. Here are some guidelines you might follow when you're dealing with people who seem to consider only themselves:

**Don't offer a compromise when you know that its limits won't be respected.** You'll probably end up doing everything that was originally asked of you and more. (This process is referred to as the "slippery slope" because it's downhill all the way.)

For example, let's say Uncle Joe wants you to spend Saturday helping him paint his house. If you're busy (or just don't want to spend your day that way), you could offer to come for a couple of hours in the morning. This could be a great way to offer some help while still respecting your own needs – if Uncle Joe is reasonable. But if he has a way of talking you into things you don't want to do, it may be better not to go at all. Be polite but firm:

> *Sorry, Uncle Joe, I won't be able to help this weekend.*
> *"Why not?"*
> *I've already made plans.*
> *"Can't you change them for me?"*
> *No, I can't.*

If you still want to help, consider arriving late in the day, when there are only a few working hours left. This allows you to be helpful while ensuring that your limits are respected.

**Don't make a sacrifice this time in the hope that it will be returned in the future.** Unreasonable people seldom reciprocate. And when they do, it's on their terms (which generally include you making further sacrifices).

One of the parents in the carpool wants you to take her place on Friday. Friday is a busy day for you, but you could change your schedule to accommodate her. You know from experience, however, that when it's time for her to reciprocate, she always has an excuse. Don't tell yourself that she'll be there for you some time when you need it; you already know better. Accept the fact that she won't return the favor (unless she wants something else from you), and take this into account when you make your decision.

**Don't base your decision on any expectation that the person will do what's right.** Unreasonable people don't share your ideas about fairness; that's part of what makes them unreasonable. They seldom, if ever, admit to mistakes – and therefore see no need to make things right. They've also mastered the art of finger-pointing. Placing responsibility on everyone but themselves means they don't need to do anything that doesn't fit their agenda.

**Most importantly, do not attempt to reason with these people.** Keep your explanations to a minimum or, better yet, don't explain at all. Unreasonable people, by definition, cannot be expected to accept a reasonable argument. So don't argue. Don't explain. Don't justify. State your decision firmly:

*No, I won't be chairing the committee for this year's fundraiser.*
*"But why not? We've always relied on you to get the job done!"*
*I know. That's why I'm letting you know now ... while there's plenty of time to find someone else.*

When dealing with these people, remind yourself (repeatedly if necessary) that you do not need to prove yourself to anyone. Providing excuses or over-explaining puts the other person in charge of both the conversation and your feelings about yourself. Excuses will lead to endless debate – until you're so exhausted that you'll agree to just about anything. Simple statements are best:

*I won't be there.*
*You'll need to ask someone else this time.*
*I'm sorry, but I have too many commitments right now.*

When asked why you won't be there or what's so important, consider one of these noncommittal responses:

*I simply can't make it.*
*I just have too much on my plate already.*
*I'm overbooked, and everything on my list is important.*

Of course, what matters is that you're comfortable with what you're saying and you're not giving your power away by making excuses.

For more ideas on how to stop justifying yourself, see the next book in this series, *7 Easy Ways to Say NO to Almost Anyone: Stand Up for Yourself Without Looking (or Feeling) Unreasonable, Uncaring or Unkind*. The chapter on excuses and justifications provides many ways to respond without explaining too much. It also contains more information on the often-unconscious beliefs and emotions that drive us to make excuses in the first place.

## Authority

Always consider who has the authority in the relationship. No matter how much you dislike doing something, your boss may have the authority to tell you to do it. (If this happens too often, you're in the wrong job!) Your older brother may speak as if he has authority over you – but unless you're living in his basement, he doesn't!

Some people, like government officials, have authority because society has given it to them. Since society is bigger and stronger than we are, the government does have power over us. We also give others (like our bosses) authority in exchange for something we value (like a salary).

You may think that's the end of it … but often it's not. Once you start to look, you may discover that you've given a number of people power over you.

For example, you may respect someone's knowledge so much that you allow his or her opinions to outweigh your own – even when you know better. You may defer to your husband about money or to your wife about parenting. Or you may give in to people who speak with an air of authority because you find them so convincing. Often their only real advantage over you is their confidence.

There was a time when many mothers fed their babies on a schedule because their doctors told them to. They often felt uncomfortable, preferring to feed them whenever they were hungry. But they trusted their doctors' instructions more than their own common sense, so they did as they were told. They gave their doctors the authority to override their own inner knowing.

You're an adult now. Question authority. Don't give your power away like candy, and be clear on its limits. Just because you admire someone's people skills doesn't mean that his stock market advice will be good. Make conscious choices about who influences your decisions and under what circumstances.

---

> You're an adult now.
> Question authority.

---

In some cases, you may be the one with the authority (and the accompanying responsibility). You may be a parent, a boss or the head of a committee. If people like all your decisions all the time, it's probably because you're doing their bidding. Consider how much you're doing (or giving up doing) to keep others happy, and take a good, hard look at how that's working for you. To get what's important to you, you'll need to take your own priorities into account – and enforce them when necessary.

Become conscious of the authority dynamic in your relationships. Be aware of the power you give to others as well as the power they give to you (or that you allow them to withhold from you). Understand what's going on, and take that understanding into account when you make your decisions.

## Take Your Time

Remember not to let anyone rush you. If you're not used to thinking this way, take the time you need to consider the person or people you're dealing with. Put off your decision if you need to. You'll feel better about yourself, your choices, and your relationships.

# CHAPTER 3

# THE THIRD KEY: UNDERSTAND THE CONSEQUENCES OF NOT SETTING A BOUNDARY

Often it seems easier not to set a boundary – to just "go with the flow" and make everyone happy. Before you decide to go along just to keep the peace, consider the long-term consequences. Let's look at some of the pitfalls of going along "just this once."

## 1. You may be the only one who sees it that way.

For you, it's "just this once." But to everyone else, this responsibility is now yours. Those who created the problem are celebrating: they've finally found someone to take it off their hands!

Your best friend can take on too much, knowing you'll be there to bail her out. Your co-worker knows you'll cover for her when goes home early. And your family knows you'll be there; they can leave everything to you.

It's nice to be so important, but is it worth the price? What about your own life?

## 2. The expectations don't end here.

This is the "slippery slope" that I mentioned earlier. Once you agree to plan your parents' anniversary party, you may be expected to buy the decorations, store them at your house, and be there two hours ahead of time to set up. (And don't forget the clean-up!) So if you're willing to plan the party, be clear about whom you're handing off to as well as when and how. If there's no agreement on who that will be … look in the mirror. There's only one logical choice.

## 3. You exhaust yourself.

If you're the helpful type, you may find yourself tired at the end of the day … every day. You may wonder where the time has gone. I'll tell you where it's gone: to other people's wants and needs.

> If you want a rewarding life, you'll have to do the work yourself.

Can you relate? Then don't you think it's time to focus on your own life? No one will do that for you, no matter how many people you support, assist or rescue. Only you know what's important to you, and only you can make the necessary commitment. If you want a rewarding life, you'll have to do the work yourself.

## 4. You lose the respect of others.

Failing to set a boundary can result in others not taking you seriously. If you're always the one working late, even when the job is someone else's, you may soon be taken for granted. Others will learn that they can ignore their responsibilities and you'll do the work for them.

If you thought your loyalty and work ethic would earn you a leadership position, think again. Leaders inspire others to excel and remove the obstacles to their success. They don't do their work for them.

And don't think it's any different with your family or friends. When you let people take advantage of you, it easily becomes a habit. You may quickly become the only one who takes your mother to appointments or does the cooking for family dinners. While you'll probably receive plenty of kudos at first, you may soon find that no one is available when you need help. In other words, your time and effort are neither respected nor appreciated. They're assumed. Before you agree to anything, consider putting some boundaries in place:

*I'm happy to do the cooking this weekend. Who's going to clean up?*

*I can take Mom shopping and to the hairdresser if the rest of you handle everything else.*

*Actually, I cooked last weekend. Who's next?*

Generally speaking, others will only respect you when you respect yourself.

## 5. You lose your self-respect.

In the previous examples, how would it feel to be doing all the work, without any help from your brothers and sisters? After months (or years) of this, how do you think you'll feel about yourself? Would you feel valued? Important? Worthwhile? Or would your unwillingness to stand up for your own needs leave you feeling like a nobody?

Letting others take advantage of you takes its toll. You give yourself the message that you don't matter. When others treat you as unimportant, you feel unimportant ... until you put a stop to it. When you stand up for yourself, you feel important again. You feel respected and valued – by the person whose opinion matters most.

## 6. You feel angry and resentful.

When you fail to set the boundaries that are right for you, the boundaries dictated by **your** values and **your** beliefs, you end up resenting others. For example, if you believe in honesty but agree to tell a "little white lie" for your sister, you'll end up resenting her for it. If you do all the cooking or all the driving, how can you possibly feel loving toward your brothers and sisters who aren't making the effort? You can't.

But consider this: Who's responsible for these feelings? It's not someone else's value system that was violated; it's yours. It wasn't your sister who told the lie; it was **you**. And it's you – not anyone else – who feels taken for granted. So stand up for yourself. Because if you don't, you'll be left with a lot of unpleasant feelings. And – trust me on this one – they won't go away.

## 7. You lose your integrity.

Integrity is all about internal consistency. If we violate a principle that we believe in, we're out of integrity. Expecting someone to do something that we wouldn't do ourselves also takes us out of integrity.

When you tell that "little white lie," resentment isn't your only problem. When your actions aren't consistent with your values, you won't feel good about yourself. You've broken your own rules; you've failed to meet your internal standard.

It doesn't matter what anyone else believes about your actions; what matters is what **you** believe. Giving in to someone against your better judgment takes you out of integrity. And that never feels good.

## 8. You say *no* to something important.

Saying *yes* to other people's demands means saying *no* to something else. Sometimes all you're saying *no* to is a quiet evening at home. If you've had more than your share of those lately, you've probably made a good decision. But if you haven't had one in weeks, saying *yes* to someone else means saying *no* to some much-needed quiet time.

Before you say *yes*, consider the other side of the coin. What might you be saying *no* to?

## Remember ...

These are only some of the possible consequences of failing to set the boundaries that are right for you. And, of course, not all of them will happen. When deciding whether to "go with the flow" or "just say *no*," always consider the likely consequences. And remember that the emotional consequences may be the most important ones of all. Don't trade your self-respect for approval or flattery. These little "gifts" are fleeting; the resentment and low self-esteem that come along with them are far more lasting.

# CHAPTER 4

# THE FOURTH KEY: KNOW WHAT'S MISSING

Have you ever felt like something's not right, but you don't know what it is? Often we don't know what's wrong because something is missing. Everything looks OK – because the problem can't be seen.

Often when people convince us to do something, they don't tell us the whole story. They leave out the kind of information that would lead us to refuse. The better they know us, the easier this becomes. As many parents know, teenagers are masters of this art!

Let's look at some of the important information that may be missing when someone asks you for help.

## The True Size of the Task

Some things sound pretty simple: "Would you mind taking my kids home from daycare this afternoon? One of my biggest clients insisted on meeting with me today; it threw everything off." You were happy to help your sister out, even though it meant changing your own schedule. That is, until she called to say that she wouldn't be able to get home for another two hours.

You know who lets these kinds of things happen and who doesn't. Think twice before doing a favor for someone like this.

## Recurring Problems

This is another way that the job may be bigger than you thought. Perhaps your sister was at home when you got there, and you could get on with the rest of your day. When she calls twice this week looking for the same favor, you might suspect that she's taken on too much – and hoping that you'll pick up the slack. If you're happy to do it, that's great – but make sure you really are happy, and not just trying to avoid saying *no*. Think about where this could lead. How often are you willing to do this for her? How much notice do you need?

She's your sister, and you have more free time than she does – after all, you have no children and she's a divorced mother of three. So doing this for her may seem like a no-brainer. Her needs are so much greater than yours – and, honestly, you don't know how she does it. You may be inclined to do whatever you can for her, whenever you can. But if you let her needs dictate your schedule, you may find yourself resenting her – and the kids as well.

So think about what's right for you. Decide what you're willing to do, and under what conditions. And think about what, if anything, you'd like in return. The more you do, the more imbalanced the relationship becomes. These imbalances create tension.

Only you know what's right for you, so only you can make these decisions. Make them early on – before your relationship, and your self-respect, is damaged.

## The Involvement of Others

A friend has asked you to accompany her to a dinner party. You assume she wants you there because everyone else will be bringing a guest and she's not comfortable on her own. She "forgets" to mention that her ex-husband will be there. You hate him, and the feeling is mutual. While you tend to avoid people you don't like, he isn't so shy. You do **not** want to be part of this evening.

Before you agree to spend your time with people you don't know, ask a few questions. *Will anyone I know be there? How long is the event? How will people be spending their time?* (Will it be dinner and drinks, dancing, conversation, or listening to long speeches?) Perhaps it's a cocktail party, complete with designated drivers, and you don't enjoy being around people who've been drinking. Make sure you understand what's involved before you make any promises.

## The Money

This issue has already been mentioned in the previous key. If you've been asked to plan a party for someone close to you, be clear on who's footing the bill. You can approach this diplomatically by asking: *What's your budget?* Note the use of the word *your* in this question. This lets the person know your expectations without making an issue of it. (Of course, not everyone responds to diplomacy. Don't try this with someone who's likely to "misunderstand" you.)

If you're concerned about spending money and not being repaid, but you still want to plan the party, don't go shopping alone. Arrange for the person who has asked for your help to go with you, so that you won't need to pay for anything. (If you're worried, consider leaving your credit cards and most of your cash at home.) If he or she is busy, or suggests that whatever you choose is fine, make it clear that you're not comfortable spending other people's money. You must go together.

If you're asked to pick up things at the last minute, consider declining. Or ask for cash to cover the cost. (A simple *I don't want to put this on my credit card* should suffice.) An ounce of prevention is worth a pound of cure.

## Invisible Obligations

You've been asked to head up the fundraiser for your daughter's softball team. It will be over in a month, and this is a quiet time for you. It looks like an easy decision. Don't take this on without asking some important questions:

*Exactly what does this involve?*
*Once the event is over, is there anything else I'd be expected to do?*
*How will the money be handled?*

The first question is a big one. Is this their first fundraiser? Will you be expected to figure out how to raise the funds, or has that decision been made? Are there enough volunteers, or will you be recruiting them as well? (Be prepared to walk away if there aren't enough volunteers.)

The next questions will matter more to some people than others. Perhaps you're comfortable with a one-off project, but not with an ongoing responsibility. Or perhaps you're happy to organize, but you don't want to deal with the money. Don't make assumptions; ask. People will respect you for ensuring that you only make commitments you're prepared to keep.

Sometimes people keep the details from you because they're afraid you'll say *no*. But more often they don't mention things because they don't think about them. The details often seem obvious to others – particularly when they have more experience with something than you do. So ask. These kinds of questions show that you're giving the request the thoughtful consideration it deserves. Anyone who doesn't appreciate that is unlikely to appreciate you ... or your boundaries.

## Unexpected Challenges

Your aunt has a guest for the week. She's asked you to invite her to dinner on the weekend. You're having some friends over for a barbecue, so you're happy to oblige. Here's what's missing:

The visitor is a vegan, and she's shy. Your aunt has run out of ideas for both food and conversation. Her solution: ask everyone she knows to have her over on the weekend so she can get a break.

What's happening here? Instead of solving the problem directly, your aunt is looking for others to share the pain. She's not mentioning the challenges for fear of being refused. Some appropriate questions might be:

> *I'm having a barbecue with some friends. Will she be comfortable in a small crowd?*
> *Does she have any special dietary requirements?*
> *My friends will be here for the afternoon; I need to be free at 4:30. Will that work?*
> *I'll be busy getting ready – and busy afterwards. Does she have a car, or will you be taking her back and forth?*

The problem with missing information is that you don't know what's missing. With some people, we don't need to ask much. People who know how to solve their own problems don't send them our way – although it's always a good idea to be clear on your limits (like needing to be finished by 4:30). But with people who are less reliable, or with whom we have less experience, it's important to ask. Good communication can prevent all kinds of problems. And prevention is definitely the easier route.

## Why You?

Sometimes you're a good fit for the task. If you have great organizational skills, you may be asked to head up committees or projects regularly. If you have more time than others, you may find yourself doing things that take a while. If you're a fantastic cook, you may end up making most of the food when your family gets together. There's nothing wrong with any of that, as long as you're happy with what you've been asked to contribute.

But sometimes you're chosen for your willingness to say *yes* without asking too many questions. So remember to ask before you agree to anything – or be prepared to suffer the consequences.

## A Brief Reminder

Remember to ask questions and state your limits:

*What exactly is involved? Are you sure that's all?*
*Who takes over from there?*
*How long will it take?*

*I can do … but not …*
*I'm only available until …*

Make sure that everyone understands what is and is not involved. Clear communication will allow you to avoid many potential problems.

# CHAPTER 5

# THE FIFTH KEY: STAMP OUT THOSE LIES

*It is always the false that makes you suffer: the false desires and fears, the false values and ideas, the false relationships between people. Abandon the false and you are free of pain; truth makes happy, truth liberates.*
– Nisargadatta Maharaj

Truth does liberate – when it becomes our own. So let's look at some of the lies that imprison us, encouraging us to make bad choices. I cannot offer to change your truth for you, but I can give you plenty to think about. Sometimes that's enough.

## I have an obligation.

Often we believe that we're obligated to do something, even when doing it feels wrong. Sometimes fulfilling an obligation feels right – like when we pay off a car loan or help our children with their homework. But sometimes it doesn't.

Recommending your brother-in-law for a job that he's not qualified for won't feel good. And neither will lending money to someone who's unlikely to pay it back (unless giving it away somehow makes you happy).

Roles do not trump values. And neither do favors. Let's look at favors first.

---

> A favor isn't a favor
> if you owe something in return.
> That's a business transaction.

---

According to *The Free Dictionary*, a favor is "a gracious, friendly, or obliging act that is freely granted." Notice the word *freely*. A favor isn't a favor if you owe something in return. That's a business transaction. Of course, that doesn't mean you don't want to repay the other's kindness. The real question is: On whose terms? Who decides how you express your gratitude?

The clear answer is you. If you've already agreed to do something, then on some level the terms are yours. (At least, they are now.) If you made a deal that allowed the other person to decide what you will do in return – well, then, you agreed to that. If you've made no such agreements, why would you allow someone to dictate your choices?

If you're having a hard time with this question, you may find the next key, *Recognize the Emotions That Stop You in Your Tracks*, quite helpful.

Returning a favor should not require you to violate your values or compromise your relationships. Nor should it require you to seriously inconvenience yourself and those around you. You may have other reasons to do these things – reasons that go beyond your sense of obligation. That's another matter entirely. But it's important to clearly understand why you're considering something that doesn't feel good. Only then can you make the decision that's best for you.

It's up to you to decide what to do for others – according to your own values and beliefs. If someone tries to pressure you into doing something you don't want to do, it may be time to question the nature of that relationship. If you're being manipulated, you may need to walk away ... or at least stop allowing it. If you can't even imagine doing that, please consider counseling or other professional assistance. You need to deal with the painful emotions and beliefs that have been holding you back so that you can get on with your life.

And what about roles? Is there an adult in your life for whom you feel responsible? Perhaps you feel that, as a mother, it's your job to support your children. When they come to you for money, you give it to them; you feel it's your duty. But is it?

Once your children are grown, it's their turn to take responsibility for themselves and their children. Do you regularly give them money that you'd rather spend on yourself – or allow yourself to be used as a full-time babysitter – because you'd feel guilty saying *no*? Or is it because you like feeling important to them? (We all like to feel needed at times.) We'll explore these questions in the next key. For now, think about why you make the choices you do … and ask yourself how well they're working for you. You may be happy with some, but not with others.

A healthy sense of obligation comes from either (a) gratitude for someone's kindness or (b) not having completed your part of an agreement. If yours doesn't, I encourage you to explore it further. Find out why you feel so obligated, and ask yourself what it is that you believe you owe. How will you know when the debt is paid?

Please don't rely on anyone other than yourself for this; the world is full of people who would love for you to believe that your obligation to them can never be repaid. (Some of them are our children and parents.) Every obligation has its limits. Find those limits and insist on respecting them.

If you'd like to read a bit more on obligation, see the chapter on handling manipulation directly in *7 Easy Ways to Say NO to Almost Anyone*. It also contains some great responses to guilt trips.

## But then I won't be a good person.

Some of us have been brought up to believe that good people always put others first, even when that means ignoring their own needs. We often learn this from a parent or other important role model. We are taught in words ("Never say *no* to someone who needs your help") and, even more powerfully, by example. If you were raised by someone who put everyone else first – and was praised for doing so – you may find it difficult to do things differently. You may feel as though you're letting that parent down, or at least failing to live up to the standard that he or she set.

---

> Trying to be a carbon copy of someone is no way to live.

---

It's important to realize that always putting others first is an unhealthy way to live. Do it for long enough and you will have no life – and no energy left to help those who matter most to you. Deciding to take your own needs into account isn't failing to meet the standard; it's setting a higher one. You're not letting that other person down; trying to be a carbon copy of someone is no way to live. Refuse to let **yourself** down. Make a commitment to consider your own needs along with everyone else's.

Saying *no* may make you a bit less popular, but it does not make you a bad person. Good people have needs, too. And the smart ones look after them.

## Their needs are more important.

When viewed in isolation, it may seem that others' needs are more important than your own – particularly if they lead busier lives than you do. You're single, and your brothers and sisters all have children. They're simply too busy to help look after your mother – even though you've been there with her every day since she got sick last month. How can you ask them for help, when they're so busy with their families? And, besides, if they had the time they'd offer … right?

The truth is that you **can** ask – and not everyone offers. Your brothers and sisters may not understand how much work is involved or how hard it is on you. Many people assume that you'll ask for help when you need it. And others are too busy with their own problems to notice yours.

If you've taken on too much, there are lots of ways to ask for help. You could call a family meeting, in person or by phone or internet. You could contact your brothers and sisters individually and ask for help. You could ask for something specific, or ask them each what assistance they can offer. Or you could make a list of everything you're doing and ask everyone to take over something. (A list can make a powerful statement about the need for assistance –

and remind you of how much you've taken on.) How you go about it will depend on your needs and your relationship with your family. The most important thing is that you do it. If you don't respect your own needs, you can't expect anyone else to do it for you.

## When you love someone, it's up to you to make that person happy.

The truth is that no one can make another person happy. We simply do not have that kind of power. Yes, your decisions will affect those close to you. Your son will be thrilled if you buy him a new car for his 18th birthday. Your spouse may not like it if you sign up for an evening course. But in the grand scheme of things, their reactions are fleeting. These choices will neither bring them lasting happiness nor take it away.

Happiness is not a drug that can be administered by others. It's an overall state of mind, and one that isn't easily affected by temporary gains and losses. It comes from within. Some people are happy; some are not. No one has the power to change that in another person. We may be able to bring a smile to someone's face or encourage a friend to see things more positively in the moment. But our overall state is created through our own choices, not someone else's.

The truth is that you are not responsible for anyone's feelings but your own. (And even then, you can't control them. You simply choose how to deal with them.) All you can do for others is to treat them with respect and consider their wants and needs. Part of that respect can be to allow them to experience feelings like disappointment without trying to rescue them.

It is not your job to save others from their disappointment, hurt or anger. These are all part of the human experience, something that we all must deal with. A child who has is protected from these emotions will have a tough time when he experiences them as an adult. It is neither healthy nor wise to treat painful emotions as dangers that must be avoided at all costs.

> It is not your job to save others from their disappointment, hurt or anger.

The best thing you can do for others is to treat them with respect; let them know that you care about them without subjugating your needs to theirs. When you acknowledge that you're not responsible for anyone else's state of mind, you're free to make choices that are aligned with your highest values. This often turns out to be best for everyone else as well.

## This little thing isn't worth fighting over.

Of course, this is true sometimes. You're in the mood for pizza, but your friends prefer Chinese. Most likely you'll get over it and enjoy the evening with your friends. But often something far more important is at stake. Let's look at the lies that may be hidden within this simple idea.

First of all, this "little thing" may not be so little. When you're evaluating a potential boundary, it's important to be very clear on *everything* that you're dealing with. When someone continually threatens you with rejection or any other form of loss (money, status, etc.), the actual demand may seem quite small. Place it in the larger context of your ongoing relationship before you decide how to respond. How many similar demands have there been? Are there likely to be more? Is the demand or the way it's expressed disrespectful? Is someone trying to intimidate you? These questions can help you to see whether you're dealing with one little thing, one significant thing, or a larger pattern of disrespect.

Now place it in the context of your highest values and beliefs. What does it mean to you to give in to the latest demand? Chances are there's a lot more at stake: your integrity and self-respect. It's time to take a good, hard look at what you expect to lose ... and what you'll gain by setting and maintaining a boundary. Consider the personal cost before you make any decision. It's often far greater than any aspect of the immediate situation.

Now that we've redefined this "little thing" to include your integrity, it's easy to see why it might be worth fighting for. But you're probably under the impression that the battle you've been avoiding is between you and someone else. Think again. The greatest conflict by far will be the one that takes place within yourself. And although it may be painful, it is well worth the discomfort. Learning to respect yourself is one of the most important things you'll ever do.

This inner struggle may take some time; don't give up if you find you're not able to change overnight. Be persistent and you will succeed.

Once you've won the inner battle, you may find that the outer one seems almost trivial. When you make a commitment to yourself and your values, everyone around you can sense it. Often people will back off when they see that you've changed. And those who don't will become far easier to deal with once you're sure of yourself. Even if their behavior escalates, your emotions don't have to. Your commitment to respecting yourself gives you both strength and perspective.

## It's better to keep the peace.

Your grandfather is making racist comments … again. Changing the subject or quietly withdrawing from the conversation may be your best option. Keeping the peace does have its place. But sometimes we know there's more at stake – and we still choose to avoid conflict.

We'll discuss the possible emotions behind these decisions in the next key, but for now let's stick to beliefs and values. Some people believe that harmony within a group, especially a family, is more important than their own needs. For many, this is the key to fulfilling relationships. This is no problem ... until they feel they must choose between respecting themselves and maintaining that perceived harmony.

When relationships are based on trust and mutual respect, this level of sacrifice is never required. If the relationships in a group have deteriorated to this point, no amount of self-sacrifice will revive them. Disrespecting anyone, including yourself, will only reinforce the existing dynamic.

In this case, the lie has to do with the nature of peace. There is none here, only a lack of obvious conflict. The next threat to this "peace" could come at any moment; it is neither lasting nor genuine. Real peace will only be achieved when the group dynamic changes. Trust and respect must be restored.

In a situation like this, giving in only makes things worse. The sooner the current situation is challenged, the sooner things can improve. Treat everyone, including yourself, with respect – and encourage others to do the same. **This** is the foundation of lasting peace. It also takes courage and integrity, so expect setbacks as well as successes. Keep at it until it becomes automatic.

## There's nothing I can do.

It's human nature to give up when our repeated efforts don't get us anywhere. ("She won't take *no* for an answer! What am I supposed to do?") It's also human to try the same approach repeatedly, with only minor variations. Doing the same thing over and over, but expecting different results, is a common definition of insanity

When the situation feels helpless, it's usually because you've accepted the role of victim. You've lost track of your true power. As we'll see in the final key, your strength lies in acceptance. Once you accept that the other's decisions and behavior will not change – and reject the role of victim – you'll see the benefits of changing your response.

If someone truly won't take *no* for an answer, all the excuses and cajoling in the world won't change that. So stop. Take your power back:

*I'm sorry you feel that way. Next time give me a bit more notice and I'll see what I can do.*

If the harassment continues, walk away (or hang up the phone, or don't respond to the email).

Even if you can't change someone else's decision, you can still reject the role of victim. Let's imagine that your spouse has made plans for Saturday, forgetting that it's your birthday. The money is not refundable; you've been told that cancellation is not an option. How do you reject the role of victim?

Once you get through the emotions and accept the situation (which may take a while), you're free to decide how else you might like to spend your

Saturday. Are there friends you would like to see? Is there something you would enjoy doing that your spouse isn't interested in? A woman might want to spend some time at a spa with one of her friends. A man might want to play golf. A nature lover might want to spend the day hiking or birdwatching. You could celebrate with your partner on Sunday, making the entire weekend a birthday celebration.

And if you feel hurt, it may be time to take a serious look at your relationship. If your spouse isn't interested in your needs, perhaps the two of you have some issues to resolve. See this as a wake-up call and give your relationship the attention it needs. And if you've done that already, choose your next steps consciously. Every relationship is based on choices.

When you take back your power, things change for the better. Even if you're still unhappy with the situation, you'll feel better about yourself. Accepting the role of victim can leave you feeling bitter, resentful and weak. Rejecting that role will bring you strength and confidence. So often we wait until we feel confident enough to stand up for ourselves; we have it all backwards. Standing up for ourselves, even in small ways, is how we gain that confidence in the first place.

So remember: Even if you can't get everything you want right now, there's still something that you can change.

## It's no big deal – I shouldn't feel so angry.

Anger and resentment are clues. Think of them as messages from deep within yourself. They tell you that something is wrong; unfortunately, they don't spell out the details. It's up to you to figure it out.

When someone is asking (or demanding) something of you, anger and resentment may indicate that you need to take a closer look. Perhaps some aspect of it is not in your best interest. It may be something obvious (you're tired and don't want to listen to your sister's complaints tonight) or a bit subtle (you've been disrespecting yourself by giving in to someone's implied threats).

Often we feel angry at ourselves for putting up with something that isn't right for us. At a conscious level, we direct our anger toward someone else. But underneath it all, we're angry at ourselves. Standing up for ourselves, in whatever way works best for us, will resolve that anger and set things right.

We often keep ourselves in victim mode by minimizing our feelings. *What's the big deal?* we ask. We justify our decision to put others first:

*One more late night at the office won't kill me.*
*I know how to handle my sister's complaints by now.*
*I'm a little tired, that's all.*
*My mother's lonely. She needs some company. Certainly I can miss a night out with my friends for her.*

But the body isn't so easily fooled. How do you feel when you make those excuses? Do you feel queasy? Is your face flushed? Does your throat tighten up? In other words, is this self-talk accompanied by pain or discomfort? If it is, your body is telling you something.

Maybe one more late night at the office is one more night of allowing others to take advantage of you. Continuing to do everyone else's work while they relax at home may not actually kill you, but what is it doing to your self-respect?

Putting your sister's desire to spend a few hours unloading on you ahead of your need for rest doesn't say much about your value, either. And you can see your mother tomorrow night, after your night out with your friends. After all, you only get together with them once a month. Sharing your plans with your mom and arranging another time respects both of your needs.

## They just can't manage without me.

Very few people are truly incompetent – even in a single area of their lives. They've simply discovered (sometimes unconsciously) that it's easier to rely on others than to deal with certain problems themselves. Appearing helpless is a great way to generate sympathy and assistance from others.

These people may have come to see themselves as helpless, and they may be afraid of facing challenges on their own. They may truly believe that they need you. Usually the best thing you can do for them (as well as yourself) is to encourage them to take responsibility for their own needs. Express your faith in their abilities and – if it's appropriate and you want to – consider offering some form of support. People who don't believe in themselves begin to thrive when they succeed, even at small things. If someone depends on others for too much, helping that person to take small steps can make a big difference.

Of course, some people simply find it easier to let others do the work. Trust your feelings about the person and the situation and decide how much effort you wish to invest, if any. Simply saying *no* to future requests is always an option.

I could go on for a while about how people become dependent and why they seem to want to stay that way. But if someone is consistently depending on you, it's far more useful to understand what drives you to allow that dependence. Yes, you can support others in changing … if they want to change. But the only person you have any real power with is yourself.

Sometimes we allow people to depend on us because we think we must, because this is what good people do. But there is another reason for allowing, or even subtly encouraging, dependence.

Some of us have a great desire to feel needed. It makes us feel important. When someone depends on us, we matter. And maybe without that, we feel useless and irrelevant. We'll discuss this later in the next key: *Recognize the Emotions that Stop You in Your Tracks*.

The truth is that they **can** manage without you. They aren't helpless. And you don't need to be needed. If you believe otherwise, do something about it. Because as long as you keep believing these lies, someone will use them to manipulate you.

## I can't handle the consequences.

How often do you go along with something because you believe you can't afford not to? You can't question the need to work on Saturday because your boss will think you're not committed to the project. You **need** that job.

Fear is a powerful motivator. And when we're afraid that something terrifying will happen, we'll do almost anything to stop it. Let's look at how your fears and beliefs can combine to rob you of your power.

Your boss wants you to work on Saturday ... again. You've made plans that are important to you. But cancelling them may not be necessary. It's possible that you could do the extra work at home, or stay late on Friday night or come in before or after your Saturday event. It's also possible that, since you've put in so many extra hours already, the project could manage without you for one weekend. If you assume the worst and fear losing your job, you'll cancel your plans and resent doing so. If you explore your options in a way that respects your boss's concerns, you may be pleasantly surprised.

The belief that we can't handle the consequences is always a lie. Often they aren't half as bad as we imagine them to be. And usually the real consequences are emotional; a great deal of the time we're simply running away from our own fear.

You **can** handle the consequences. You just don't want to. Learn to recognize this crucial difference.

If you find yourself doing things that feel wrong in order to avoid the pain you associate with saying *no*, consider making this your mantra:

*I **can** handle it.*
*I **can** handle it.*
*I **can** handle it.*

Then start with something small, and stand up for yourself despite your fear. You're stronger than you think. And you'll be surprised at how good you feel when you make yourself important for a change.

## But they won't like me.

So often we fail to stand up for ourselves because we're afraid of rejection. This is especially true when our parents or other authority figures are involved.

You can't tell your father that you're not going on the "family vacation" … he's already told you he won't take *no* for an answer. And, besides, the whole family will be there. How can you put your own selfish needs ahead of everyone else's?

The truth is that this vacation was planned with everyone's interests in mind but yours. It's at an expensive resort; you're not as wealthy as the rest of your family. And you don't enjoy the beach or water sports. So why would you spend so much money – and half of your annual vacation time – for the privilege of watching everyone else have fun?

Perhaps you're doing it to "keep the peace." You tell yourself that you're making a sacrifice for the greater good. But are you? Or are you doing it because you can't stand to disappoint your parents? You may be willing to do almost anything to avoid your mother's hurt look and your father's disapproving stare. But you **can** handle it. Their disappointment won't last forever. And maybe next year they'll take your interests into account, and you'll find yourself looking forward to the family trip.

## I can never break my word.

Sure, you can.

Things change. Your job gets busier. Your kids need more of your time. You can't get the support you need on the political committee you've been chairing. The student who was helping you with your housekeeping is in the hospital. The busier you are, the more often you'll need to change and adapt.

And sometimes you're just tired. A client shared this story with me: Her week was far busier than expected, and she was exhausted on the weekend. She sent a text message to say that she wouldn't be attending a Saturday afternoon barbecue. She was astounded by the reply, which went something like this: "We've had a death in the family, but we'll be there. We're expecting the salad that you promised to bring."

I guess some people really do believe that all commitments must be honored. My client is not one of those people. She chose not to respond.

For most of us, there are times when it makes sense to "uncommit." I personally like to keep my commitments, so I prefer to avoid overcommitting in the first place. But sometimes it's necessary. If you've reached that point, I recommend that you explain the reasons – briefly and simply – and apologize if appropriate. If the details are personal, and the relationship isn't, consider something a bit vague. (I like, *Something unexpected came up*, or *I'm sorry, but I need to deal with a personal emergency*.) Give the other person as much notice as possible. Your goal is to respect others' needs without trampling on your own.

Sometimes a commitment turns out to be different than expected. We base our promises on the information available at the time. If someone withholds important details, the commitment was obtained through deception. For me, being deceived means all bets are off. And if the person has deceived me before, it may mean the end of the relationship. It definitely means the end of trust.

If important information was kept from you, or the situation has changed, I encourage you to give yourself permission to "uncommit." You won't do it every time, but it's good to have your options open. Most of us do our best to keep our commitments. But your best need not include wearing yourself out – or doing things that you never would have agreed to.

## There are some people I just can't say *no* to.

In some ways, this doesn't seem like a lie at all. Perhaps there **are** some people you can't refuse. But this is simply another way of saying that you can't handle the consequences. You can say *no* to anyone. You just don't want to. Why? Because somehow you've given certain people your power.

Why do we give our power to the same people, time and time again? There are two types of reasons. Some people do things for us. They let us use their vacation home or introduce us to influential people or make us feel good about ourselves. If you find yourself doing things you don't want to do for reasons like these, be clear about what these favors are costing you.

If you're violating your own values just to please someone, you're prostituting yourself. Is the benefit you're hoping to receive worth your integrity? If you're doing things you find uncomfortable, consider whether the exchange is worthwhile. If it is, making your choices more consciously will help you to get past any resentment you may have been feeling. If it isn't, it's time to look at the relationship and decide how to proceed.

You might simply set a boundary regarding the things that don't work for you and see what happens. Or, if that wouldn't feel right to you, you might decide to accept fewer of those benefits (or even none at all). It all depends upon your values, the relationship you have now, and the relationship you want to have in the future. Take the time to consider these issues before choosing your course of action.

This strategy can also be at work even when we don't receive any actual benefits. The boss who dangles a promotion in front of you is a perfect example of this. So is the parent whose approval is at stake with every request. That approval is neither lasting nor real.

Sometimes we are motivated by the hope of gain; at other times, we want to avoid loss. Maybe your boss isn't dangling a promotion in front of you; he's telling you that everyone must work harder and longer if they want to keep their jobs. Or someone close to you has this judgmental tone that works every time; you can't deal with her disapproval. Or a friend convinces you to lie for her because you're afraid of losing her friendship. Your fear pushes you to do things that you wouldn't normally do.

In these cases, the solution lies in becoming aware of the dynamics of the relationship – and the conflicts within yourself. Once you understand what's happening – and what's at stake – you can start making choices that work for you. Until then, you're likely to be a regular victim of your emotions – particularly your fears.

## They just won't take *no* for an answer.

This may be the biggest lie of all, because it's disguised as the truth. It may be that your father won't take *no* for an answer; he insists that you be part of the family vacation. He'll pay your way if money's a problem. If he's particularly manipulative, he may even book you into the resort without your permission.

That's the part that's true. So where's the lie?

It's hidden in the idea that someone "just won't take *no* for an answer." The truth is simple: It's OK if someone refuses to accept your answer. An answer is not taken; it is given. And that answer is entirely up to you.

When someone refuses to accept your decision, he or she is in denial: denying reality and trying to deny your right to make your own choices. Your answer is your answer. Period. Others' refusal to accept it has nothing to do with you – unless, of course, you need their agreement. Then you've given them the power to make your decisions for you. (Of course, there are times when we need the agreement of someone with authority or resources. That's a different story.)

If this concept is new to you, take a moment to let it sink in. It's OK if others don't like your decisions.

Your life is not meant to be a democracy with everyone getting a vote. Do what **you** feel is right; whether others accept it or not is their business. Don't allow someone else's denial to become yours.

---

> Your life is not meant to be
> a democracy with
> everyone getting a vote.

---

*The Broken Record Technique* (explained in *7 Easy Ways to Say NO to Almost Anyone*) is a great way to deal with denial. As you might guess, it involves repeating your decision over and over – same words, same tone, same expression. It's boring but highly effective, especially when followed by walking away.

## What Are You Believing?

It is the nature of lies to lead us astray. When we believe them, consciously or otherwise, we end up doing things we wouldn't otherwise do. So before you do something you may regret, ask yourself what you're believing. And decide for yourself whether it's true.

# CHAPTER 6

# THE 6ᵀᴴ KEY: RECOGNIZE THE EMOTIONS THAT STOP YOU IN YOUR TRACKS

Before I get into the specific emotions that seem to have the most power over us, I'd like to talk about the importance of our feelings. They're the key to just about everything.

If you don't believe me, think about what's most important to you. If it's career or business success, you may think that emotion plays no part. But what makes that success so attractive? Is it the expensive house or car? The luxurious vacations? The admiration of others?

Without the emotions that come with them, you wouldn't care about these things at all. What you value is the way you **feel** when you drive the car, lie on the beach or notice others admiring you – or when you succeed at something. Or, if you're fortunate, you may enjoy the way you feel when you do your work. The journey itself brings you a sense of fulfillment.

A good life is one filled with whatever it is that you value. Money and status trigger certain feelings within us. So does being surrounded by family. Even a life of service is attractive because of the feelings we get from helping others. We value things that feel good. Our emotions cannot be disconnected from our values. And, for precisely that reason, they play a critical role in choosing, setting and maintaining our boundaries.

So let's look at the emotions that stop us from standing up for ourselves, even when we desperately want to.

## Fear of Saying *No*

For some of us, the word *no* is scary. One of my clients told me she associates *no* with rejection. She hates to hear it, and she doesn't want to say it, either. She wants nothing to do with that emotional pain.

What does the word *no* mean to you? Rejection is certainly one option. This simple little word is also associated with judgment, with being wrong, and with the consequences of standing up to someone who has power over you. Saying *no* to a parent, teacher or other authority figure could be dangerous for a child. It could lead to rejection, beatings or humiliation (or all the above). And especially when we're young, hearing it from someone important can trigger intense self-judgment. For many people, *no* means something is wrong with them; they've failed.

## Fear of Conflict

As far as I can tell, no one likes conflict. But some people experience far more fear of it than others, and they'll do almost anything to avoid that fear.

For some, even a minor disagreement feels downright dangerous. That's because, at some point in their lives, it was. Someone who grew up in a home where arguments often led to emotional or physical abuse may go to extremes to avoid even minor disagreements. These people may need someone to help them put conflict and confrontation back into perspective.

When physical safety fears aren't the issue, conflict (like the word *no*) may feel like a failure. If you've always been the peacemaker, the one who sorts out everyone else's disputes, you may see conflict as a sign that you've failed. It may trigger the painful feelings associated with not being good enough or not being in control. If making (or keeping) peace is something you do well – and fairly often – you may be avoiding conflict and confrontation out of habit, or because you don't understand that they can be good for a relationship.

If someone puts you down, you may need to confront that person – or accept that the put-downs won't stop any time soon. You may get an argument: "Can't you take a joke?" Stay firm: *I don't think it was funny. Please don't do it again.* Or you may get an apology. After all, not everyone is out to get us. Sometimes we need to tell the people we care about how we feel. This can only improve a healthy relationship.

---

> Disagreement
> does not equal rejection.

---

Conflict may also be associated with the pain of rejection. Some of us have never gotten over these hurts. Perhaps they were intense, or repeated often, when we were still too young to cope with our feelings. It's important to remind ourselves that disagreement does not equal rejection. We can disagree with the people closest to us but still love and respect them.

## Fear of Rejection

Rejection is simply an intense form of disapproval. How we handle it depends upon our childhood experiences. If we received lots of positive reinforcement during that important time, we'll feel pretty good about ourselves later on. Rejection won't have too much power over us. Many of us, though, were neglected or rejected as children. If these wounds haven't healed, the fear of rejection may be a powerful force in our lives.

Rejection may take the form of insults ("How can you be so stupid?"), other angry words ("I wish I'd never met you!") or a look that makes words entirely unnecessary. It may also manifest as the silent treatment. For some of us, being ignored brings up the pain of early abandonment. Because this unresolved pain was so intense, avoiding anything like it has become a top priority.

People who fear rejection are afraid of the past. Unresolved trauma of any nature has that power over us. We're willing to do all kinds of things to avoid the pain we fear so much – even things that go against our values. Here are some examples of the power we give to our fear of rejection:

- I've decided to lend her the money after all. If I don't, she'll never speak to me again.
- Yes, I covered for him. What else can I do? We work together; it's not like I can avoid him....
- If I even hint that I might be too busy, she'll give me that "How did I end up with you for a daughter?" look.... I just can't handle that.

## Craving the Approval of Others

For many, avoiding rejection isn't enough to keep their feelings of low self-worth at bay. They need the approval of others to feel good about themselves. If any of the following statements are true, you may fall into this category:

- You typically consider how to word your opinion so that others will agree. When that's too difficult, you're likely to keep it to yourself.
- You feel uncomfortable when others aren't happy with your decisions … but fortunately that doesn't happen too often.
- When someone asks you for help, even when it's not what you want to do, it's too hard to say *no*.
- You're willing to give up things that matter to you in order to keep the peace.
- You promise to stand up for yourself next time … but you don't.

---

Approval is a quick fix,
a way to suppress our
difficult feelings about ourselves.

---

As you may have noticed from some of these examples, there's a fine line between fearing rejection and craving approval. Fortunately the difference doesn't matter. The important thing to know is this: Approval is a quick fix, a way to suppress our difficult feelings about ourselves. But quick fixes never last, so before we know it we're looking for another one. And our power lies in the hands of anyone who can give it to us.

## Need to Be Needed

I think many people who "need to be needed" don't trust that they'll be loved for who they are. People who fear rejection or crave approval often encourage others to become dependent on them. This is their way of making sure they won't be left behind. Others may encourage dependence because it makes them feel special or important. "What would I do without you?" can be a great ego boost.

The problem with dependency is that no one enjoys it. Some people will gladly play victim to your rescuer. They may lack confidence in themselves, or they may too lazy to do the work themselves. But whether they're happy about it or not, don't expect much from someone who's become dependent on you. The victim/rescuer dynamic is hardly the foundation for a fulfilling relationship.

Feeling needed can also help us to avoid feeling powerless (which is pretty scary for most of us). When we're needed, we're in control. We make the decisions. We determine the outcome.

Many of us feel powerless in specific areas of our lives. For some it's work-related: we can't please the boss, we can't get that promotion – or we can't even find a job. For others, it's family: parents whose demands can never be met, children who are acting out or conflicts with our partners. Others may experience their lives as empty and meaningless.

Feeling needed can give us a false sense of power, security and importance. It can drown out fear, rejection, guilt and other painful emotions – but only for a little while. It's a quick fix that actually keeps us suffering.

Yes, that's right. I'll say it again: **It keeps us suffering.** You might wonder how that can be. Certainly the cure for feeling powerless is to feel powerful again ... isn't it?

No, it's not. Feeling powerful in one part of your life will not make up for feeling powerless in another.

The most effective way to deal with feeling powerless is simply this: **allow yourself to feel powerless.** Take some quiet time and simply experience it. Feel the fear, the anger, the judgment – whatever's there. It can only control you while you're running away from it. Face your feelings and everything else follows. When you change, how you relate to everything around you changes. And once that happens, your life will never be the same!

---

> Feeling powerful in one part of your life will not make up for feeling powerless in another.

---

If you're not prepared to feel emotional pain (and many people aren't), at least become aware of the ways you try to compensate – and the price you've paid for not facing it. Notice how you feel when people seem to need you – and when you believe they don't. Admit that you like to feel needed. Accept that you want to avoid the feelings that come when you think you don't matter. Just don't let that fear run your life.

As long as you're afraid of your own emotions, others can take advantage of you. Your true power lies in your willingness to experience some emotional pain when necessary. When you need to feel needed, someone else is in control. When you're willing to walk away, even if it means feeling uncomfortable for a while, you're free.

So become more aware. Look within and understand what drives your decisions. If feeling needed is too important to you, I encourage you to get some help with your emotions.

Difficult feelings are a natural part of being human. Allowing yourself to experience them (even a little bit) gives you greater power over them – and anyone who tries to use them against you.

## Guilt

Of all the emotional patterns that lead us to do things "against our will," guilt is the classic. It has been used through the ages to convince people to sacrifice their desires for someone else's. I doubt that anyone reading this hasn't done **something** out of guilt.

Healthy guilt tells us we've done something wrong (or failed to do what was right). It's a signal that we need to change our behavior in some way. It may be telling us to apologize for saying something hurtful, to pay more attention to someone in our lives, or to consider "giving back" to a world that has given us so much.

If guilt is such a good thing, why are we so easily manipulated by it? What's gone wrong?

Guilt is a deeply ingrained emotion, one which we learned at an early age. When our parents and other authority figures told us we were bad because we said something hurtful or refused to share our toys, we took that in. Over time, we developed mental and emotional patterns that protected us from emotional pain – or made us feel better about ourselves.

For some, that process has worked well. Most of the time, they act according to their higher values and feel good about their choices. When they don't, guilt pushes them to do something differently. They make amends, learn from their mistakes and get on with life.

But others feel guilty at the drop of a hat. When something goes wrong, they immediately take the blame. They hold onto their past mistakes, unable to forgive themselves for simply being human. That's why guilt trips work so well on them.

Even those with a healthy sense of self-worth can fall into the guilt trap. Many of the lies from the previous key lead us to feel guilty when it's not appropriate. A mistaken sense of responsibility often lies behind the guilt that manipulators make use of – or that we fall prey to within ourselves. We think we owe someone, we're determined to make someone happy, or we're trying to live up to an unrealistic (and unhealthy) standard.

We react emotionally, never questioning these beliefs. And we fail to ask ourselves the most important question of all: Whose values are these? Guilt is only appropriate when you've violated your own values. It tells you to stop and think about what you're doing, or what you've just done. It's a wake-up call from your unconscious mind. It's not supposed to be a life sentence.

Your sister has three daughters, and they're all busy with recitals and sports. She's a stay-at-home mom who attends every single event. She wants her children to know how important they are to her – and to everyone else in the family as well. She seems to think that because you don't have children of your own, you have plenty of time to attend their weekend activities. Whenever you try to tell her you're too busy, she reminds you of everything she's done for you – and how important it is for the children to know that you care. You end up feeling guilty and resolve to pay more attention to your nieces.

Do you see the lies here? Whatever your sister may have done for you, you are not your nieces' second mother. You do not owe it to her, or to them, to attend event after event. And missing a few recitals won't make you a bad person. Attending too many, however, may lead you to resent your sister – and even your nieces, whom you love dearly. The price is much higher than a few hours of your time. And the benefit is questionable at best. There are many ways to show your nieces how much you love them. Don't let someone else dictate how you do that.

If you feel guilty a little too often, consider reviewing the lies in the previous key, with special attention to the ones just mentioned. Question your beliefs. Notice whose values you're living by. If they're not your own, make some changes.

And consider your self-image. Do you like yourself? Do you see yourself as a good person? Or have you come to believe that nothing you do will ever be good enough, that you don't deserve the good things you have? If so, I encourage you to get the help you need. Let go of these lies. Whoever taught them to you was suffering and passed that pain onto you. There's nothing you can do to change the past. But that doesn't mean you have to live with its consequences for the rest of your life.

## Feeling Sorry for Someone

Compassion and pity are **not** the same thing. They do not lead to the same actions – or the same results. Pity keeps people in the victim role. Compassion supports them in becoming stronger.

Most of us have felt sorry for someone at one time or another. It seems to be part of our human nature to identify with the suffering of others and try to lighten the load. People who feel that impulse strongly often enter the fields of medicine or psychology, or devote their lives to a cause. Those who don't have this outlet may look for other ways to make a difference.

Be careful here. Seeing other people as victims to rescue plays into our emotional wounds. Looking after others can feel good – especially if you have an unconscious need to be needed. Taking on others' responsibilities reinforces this need; it feeds the addiction. It also encourages dependence. If you want to make a real difference, help someone to become more resilient in some way (physically, mentally, emotionally or spiritually). Offer the kind of support that, by its nature, is soon outgrown.

## Loneliness

For those who don't have enough contact with family and friends, loneliness can be a big motivator. There's nothing wrong with that; in fact, helping others is a great cure for loneliness. It's only a problem if you find yourself doing things that violate your values (even in small ways). If that's the case, I suggest you find other ways to be with people – and limit your favors to those you feel 100% comfortable with.

## All Those Emotions ...

You may be surprised at the variety of emotions that can pull you off track. Whether we like it or not, we are emotional beings. Our feelings rule us until we make them conscious – and even then, it takes practice and determination to stop giving in to the stronger ones.

Sometimes understanding what's going on within ourselves is enough ... but sometimes it isn't. We know we're being played, but we still can't take our power back. If this is happening to you, I hope you'll get some help with your emotions. Sometimes they seem a bit stronger than we are, and we need someone to help us release them.

# CHAPTER 7

# THE 7<sup>TH</sup> KEY: THE POWER OF ACCEPTANCE

Not everyone is willing to "do the right thing," and not everyone cares about our priorities. Often we assume that others share our highest values; we can't imagine it any other way. But sometimes they don't, and no amount of wishing, pretending or denying the truth will change that.

In these cases, getting what's important to you comes down to power: who has it, who recognizes it, and who uses it well. There are many sources of power, and it's important to be aware of them – in ourselves as well as others.

Sometimes power comes from a group, such as society – for example, when a police officer makes an arrest. Sometimes it is more direct; having a knife in my hand gives me the power to use it. And sometimes others have the power to make us feel so awful that we'll do almost anything to make it all go away.

The power that others can exert over us – and that we can exert over them – is all about pleasure and pain, gain and loss. Winning the lottery leads to pleasure. Being passed over for a promotion leads to pain. So where exactly does our power lie, and how do we make use of it?

Your real power doesn't come from your money, your title, or your connections. When it comes to setting and maintaining boundaries, your greatest power comes from within. This power lies in your ability to do a few simple (but seldom easy) things:

**Accept yourself.** Accepting ourselves, with all our strengths and weaknesses, is one of the greatest things we can ever do. When we judge ourselves harshly, we need other people to make us feel good (even if it's only for a little while). That gives those people power over us. Acceptance frees us from relying on others for our good feelings.

Has anyone ever been able to make you feel selfish – even when you knew better? Have you ever felt guilty for not helping someone who has not once helped you? Do you feel the need to explain yourself whenever someone doesn't like your decision? If so, you're probably suffering from self-judgment.

Other people's judgments are powerless over us unless we buy into them. If you accept yourself as you are, being labeled selfish or lazy by someone with their own agenda will not make you change your mind. You'll recognize the tactic for what it is: an attempt to manipulate you through emotional pain.

The truth is that you're human ... just like the rest of us. Human nature is full of imperfections, and your nature is no different. Expecting yourself to solve everyone's problems – or to do anything perfectly, for that matter – is both unrealistic and unhealthy. Accept your limitations, whether they're physical, mental or emotional. Stop trying to be someone or something else. You're fine the way you are. If you don't believe me, I encourage you to get some help in changing that belief. Until you do, manipulative people can – and probably will – run your life.

---

> Other people's judgments
> are powerless over us
> unless we buy into them.

---

**Accept your emotions.** Being human means experiencing emotions, and some of them will be painful. Emotion is a fundamental part of the human experience. Pretending that it isn't will **not** get you the results you want (unless you enjoy unconsciously sabotaging yourself). When you see that feeling guilty, scared or inferior won't kill you, you can stop running away from those feelings. And when you do, you discover that you're more powerful than you thought. People who trigger your most painful feelings no longer control you. You are free to make choices based on your beliefs and values – choices that work for **you**.

Have you ever agreed to something just to end a conversation? If so, you were probably trying to avoid the pain that was welling up within you. Perhaps you felt angry at the person for not taking *no* for an answer. Perhaps you felt powerless; you'd explained your perfectly valid reasons time and again, but the other person wouldn't listen. Or perhaps you wanted someone to agree with you, to tell you that it's OK – and that didn't happen.

You gave in because you felt tired; unresolved emotion can be exhausting. You gave in because you wanted "it" (that awful feeling) to stop. And it did … or did it?

Although the conversation is over, you still feel angry and powerless. Not only was he unreasonable, but he overpowered you. He got what he wanted at your expense. With the conversation behind you, you're free to suppress your anger any way you like (eating, smoking, exercising, working – whatever distraction you choose). But it's still there, right below the surface … just waiting for next time.

She never did agree with you, never told you it was OK. So you gave in. Now you have her approval … but how do you feel about yourself? Whatever good feelings you might have gained have already been replaced by anger and disappointment. You didn't stand up for yourself. You didn't treat your needs as important. You feel worthless because you haven't acknowledged your own value. That's the price you pay for running away from difficult feelings. If you ask me, it's too high.

**Accept others' choices.** When we refuse to accept that others are the way they are – in other words, when we refuse to accept reality – we lose our power. We're so busy trying to change the other, or telling ourselves why the other **must** change, that we don't take action. By denying reality, we lose our ability to make choices that work for us.

Imagine that every time you go to a family gathering, your uncle drinks too much and argues loudly with anyone who will listen. You and other members of your family have asked him to stop more times than you can remember. Yet his behavior continues. So where is your power?

As long as you're expecting him to stop, your power is squarely in your uncle's hands. You want him to change; you want him to keep his pain to himself. But it's been two years now, and he hasn't changed. Wishing (or even demanding) won't make it so.

So if your power is with your uncle, how do you get it back? The first step is to accept that he will continue to act this way – and there's nothing you can do about that. He's in pain, and he's simply not going to keep it to himself. When you accept this reality, the next step comes naturally. You ask yourself what you want to do differently. If you want a different result, someone or something must change. Clearly it won't be him. So what are your options?

At a large enough gathering, you could probably avoid your uncle. Or you could find other ways to connect with your family and skip the big get-togethers. You and your family could decide not to invite him to future events until he gets some help with his drinking problem. You could even decide not to have alcohol when you get together – quite a change for some families!

On a more compassionate note, you could consider finding out what's so hard for your uncle (if you don't know already) and trying to help. Has he been this way since he lost his job? Since his wife died? What's happened to him, and what might help him to deal with his emotions? Is therapy an option? What about a support group?

Once you accept reality, you realize that you do have choices. You respond consciously rather than simply reacting in the moment.

**Accept others' opinions of you.** Not everyone will be happy when you say *no* to them in order to say *yes* to yourself. Some people will try to manipulate you by judging you and your choices.

When you consider what goes into an opinion, you see that most of them don't matter. Few people know you or your situation well enough to rate your decisions. And even fewer can put their own desires aside and see things from a balanced perspective. We tend to form our opinions of others based on little more than our own emotional experience. If they make us feel good, they must be OK. If they don't, something must be wrong with them. At the end of the day, it's all about us.

Most of the time, your opinion of someone you don't know so well says far more about you than it can ever say about him. And, by the same token, your sister-in-law's opinion of you says more about her than anyone else. How would your life be if you lived this truth? How many decisions would you change? How much better would you feel about yourself?

**Accept, accept, accept.** In other words, true power lies in acceptance – in making peace with what is rather than trying to change it. Changing reality (particularly in the form of someone else's choices) is not an effective strategy. Other people have their own beliefs, values and issues. There is nothing you can do to change any of that.

But how can you accept reality when it's so wrong? After all, your brother can't keep lying like that and your uncle needs to stop getting drunk and yelling at everyone. It's just not right!

The answer is simple. Accepting that something is the way it is does **not** mean liking it or encouraging it to continue. It simply means letting go of the idea that it must change. Stop resisting reality. People (and most situations) are as they are. No amount of "shoulding" will change them.

As you might imagine, acceptance may not come easily, even when you realize how much you need it.

But like any new habit, it requires persistence. Stick with it until you get it right.

Once you accept what is, you are free to respond to it in whatever way is best for you. You can tell your brother you won't lend him any more money – and you're not going to talk about it again. You can walk away from your uncle when he starts yelling. When that acquaintance complains about how hard life is, you can change the subject – or leave.

Responding consciously will always lead to a better result, whether out in the world or within yourself. At the very least, you'll feel better about yourself when you make a conscious choice. You may not be thrilled with the result; not everyone will gracefully accept your choices. But you'll feel more comfortable with your decision. You'll know you made it based on your own beliefs and values rather than giving in to your emotions. And you may even learn that getting what you want is easier than you thought. You'll never know until you try!

# CHAPTER 8

# SOME FINAL WORDS: DECIDE FOR YOURSELF

The same choice isn't best for everyone, even in seemingly identical situations. That's why following someone else's advice is so risky. If that person shares your most important values – or knows you well enough to understand where you differ – the advice may fit you perfectly. But if not, you risk living your life according to someone else's standards. This is a recipe for misery.

So remember the seven keys and start making use of them in your life:

1. Get to know yourself better. Be clear on your highest values, your likes and dislikes, your beliefs and your strengths and weaknesses. Better boundaries take all of this into account.
2. Think about the people you're dealing with. Are they reasonable? Do they care about you? Do they have authority over you, or do you feel you owe them? These factors affect your choices; it's time to look at them consciously.

3. Don't be too quick to go along. Resist the temptation to give others what they want so you can avoid confrontation or disapproval. This is not a good trade-off; your priorities and your self-respect are too important.
4. Look a little deeper. Don't make commitments until you understand what's really involved. How big is the job? Will doing it once be enough? And what about the financial side – are there any surprises lurking there? Get the details before you make someone else's problems your own.
5. Consider your beliefs carefully. What does it mean to be a good person? Where does your responsibility begin and end? Is it worth some sacrifice to keep the peace, or will that only allow the manipulation to continue? And remember that when someone won't take *no* for an answer, that's OK. Give it anyway.
6. Notice how you feel when you need to set a boundary. We all want to feel loved and needed, no one likes arguments, and it's all too easy to fall for a guilt trip. If these kinds of issues are driving your decisions, it's time to take back your power.
7. Catch yourself expecting things (or people) to be different. Some people are unreasonable; expecting them to change is unrealistic. So is expecting yourself to be perfect. When you accept yourself and others as you are, you're

finally able to see things clearly. And that clarity makes it easier to do what's right for you.

There's one more "secret" I'd like to share. We often see ourselves as the only person willing or able to solve the world's problems. But that's seldom true. And even when it is, it's not the crisis we imagine it to be.

If you're not available, or not comfortable with what's being asked, then say so. If you are "the only one I can count on to take care of this for me," **that's the problem**. Someone needs to find other resources. You have problems of your own that need your attention.

Practice making your own decisions about how and when to help others, using your highest values as your guide. Remember to congratulate yourself when you make sure your own needs are met. Take a few moments to feel good about the help you choose to give. And leave the rest to someone else. There's a world full of people out there. Give some of them a chance to make a difference.

# WHAT'S NEXT? A MESSAGE FROM THE AUTHOR

I hope this book has given you a new perspective on boundaries. I also know that there's always more to learn. You might want to know more about manipulation tactics. You might have a hard time saying "no", even when you know it's the right thing to do. Or maybe your emotions are running the show, and you don't know how to change that.

If you'd like more – even if you're not sure what that might be – I hope you'll join my mailing list. If you do, I'll be able to share more ideas about boundaries and relationships with you. You'll also be the first to know when I release a new book or course; I often give special discounts that are only for people on my mailing list.

I hope I've convinced you to go to **www.stephsterner.com** and sign up now, so we can stay connected.

And thanks for reading. If your life isn't already filled with people who respect both you and your boundaries, I hope you find it in yourself to change that soon. You deserve to be with people who are as good to you as you are to them.

# ABOUT THE AUTHOR

Steph Sterner has spent her life challenging the status quo. As a writer, speaker and teacher, she encourages us to be true to ourselves – to live according to our highest values. This means asking the important questions: What do we believe? Do those beliefs still work for us? What do we value most? And how to do we protect what we value?

Relationships, human nature and emotions are her passion. Through years of study, research, and contemplation – and of course her work with clients and students – she's learned a lot about what makes us human.

Steph has a remarkable gift for seeing beneath the surface, recognizing the patterns we engage in every day. As a writer, she reveals these sometimes-confusing patterns in simple terms that we can all understand. Rather than give you systems or formulas to follow, she prefers to share universal principles – and lots of examples to help you to apply them for yourself.

Born in the US, Steph now lives in Johannesburg, South Africa, where she enjoys writing and speaking, working with clients and students over the internet, and spending time in the South African sunshine.

www.stephsterner.com

Made in the USA
Columbia, SC
06 October 2017